About the Auth

Canadian born Suzan St Maur has lived in the UK since childhood. After an early career start in journalism on a local newspaper, she transferred her allegiances to advertising and later became a highly successful scriptwriter in business television and live events.

Today she writes prolifically across most media for a wide variety of business communication purposes. She has also written several published books on consumer and business topics.

Suzan has ridden since she was very young; she now has the loan of a thoroughbred mare whom she rides as often as other commitments allow. She is a committee member of the BHS-affiliated Aspley Guise & District Riding Club, and writes for a variety of other equestrian publications and websites as well as editing the AG&DRC newsletter.

Suzan lives in Bedfordshire with her son and a variety of dogs and cats.

The Horse Lover's Joke Book

Over 400 gems of horse-related humour

Suzan St Maur

KENILWORTH PRESS

To Thomas,
who has been riding since he was three years old,
and long may he share my love of horses and ponies

First published in the UK in 2001 by
Kenilworth Press, an imprint of Quiller Publishing Ltd
Reprinted 2003, 2007, 2008, 2009

British Library Cataloguing in Publication Data
A catalogue record for this book is available from the British Library

ISBN 978 1 872119 39 7

Illustrations by Dianne Breeze

Design by Paul Saunders
Typesetting and layout by Kenilworth Press
Printed in Malta by Gutenberg Press Ltd

 KENILWORTH PRESS
An imprint of Quiller Publishing Ltd
Wykey House, Wykey, Shrewsbury, SY4 1JA
tel: 01939 261616 fax: 01939 261606
email: info@quillerbooks.com
website: www.kenilworthpress.co.uk

Preface

Hello, and welcome to my first collection of horse-related jokes.

As someone said to me many years ago, if you're into horses you need a sense of humour.

But joking aside, this little book is my own way of saying 'thank you' to all the wonderful ponies, cobs and horses (plus one camel) I have had the joy of owning and/or riding over the last umpty-dump years.

I would also like to pay tribute to my parents (who bought me my first pony all those years ago), Robert, my farrier (I don't mean a word of it, honest), and the Aspley Guise and District Riding Club (whose newsletter I edit and whose members I encourage to write about horses, too).

As the Aussies say, enjoy!

SUZAN ST MAUR

★ Marital bliss

The husband was complaining again. 'You're that absorbed in your horses, I'll bet you don't even remember when we got married.'

'Of course I do, darling', smiled his wife. 'It was the day after I won my first ever Medium test on Aurora.'

★ Due respects

The Master and the Huntsman were leading a small mid-week field, trotting along a grass verge to the next covert. Along the road came a funeral cortège. The Huntsman pulled his horse up and took off his cap respectfully.

'I'm pleased to see you observe old-fashioned conventions, Hartley,' said the Master, also pulling his horse up as hounds milled around expectantly. 'Not many people have such good manners these days.'

The Huntsman replaced his cap and prepared to move off again. 'Thank you, sir,' he smiled. 'But after all, we were married for twenty-eight years.'

★ Choices

'Why the sad face?' asked one of two riders out on a hack.

'My husband says I have to choose between him and my mare,' replied the second rider.

'Gosh, I'm sorry,' commented the first rider.

'So am I,' replied the second rider. 'I'm really going to miss him.'

★ Emergency

A woman in breeches and show jacket walked up to the Secretary's desk at a dressage competition, clutching a mobile phone in one hand. 'I know my time isn't for another two hours,' she said, 'but is there any chance I could do my test a bit sooner? I've just heard that my husband has been rushed into hospital with a suspected heart attack.'

★ Riddles

Why is it that if someone tells you there are one billion stars in the universe you will believe them, but if they tell you your stirrups aren't level you have to look down at them to be sure?

What breed of horse jumps higher than a house?
All breeds. Houses don't jump.

Which route should you take through the woods when riding a fizzy horse?
The psycho path.

What is a horse's favourite television soap?
Neigh-bours.

How do you make a small fortune out of horses?
Start with a large fortune.

What did the city worker say after his first ever pony trek?
I never knew anything stuffed with hay could be so hard.

Which four frogs never ever get wet?
A showjumper that refuses at the water jump.

What does every horse and rider do at exactly the same time?
Grow old.

What has four legs and can see just as well from either end?
A horse with its eyes closed.

What happens when a black horse jumps into the Red Sea?
It gets wet.

What is as big as a horse but weighs nothing?
The horse's shadow.

If a horse's feet smell and its nose runs, what's wrong with it?
It was created upside down.

If you take your horse to an hotel, where should it stay?
In the bridle suite.

What is black and white and turns cartwheels?
A piebald horse pulling a cart.

Why are horses such bad dancers?
Because they have two left feet.

Which side of a horse has more hair?
The outside.

How do you get down from a horse?
You don't. You get down from a duck.

★ Shorties

I used to run a riding school, but business kept falling off.

Some event horses are so polite that when they get to a fence, they stop and let you go over first.

★ Who's racing?

An elderly gentleman finally achieved his lifelong ambition and bought a race horse. But it didn't seem to have much energy, so the old man got the vet in to look at him.

'This horse is very old,' said the vet.

'But will I be able to race him?' asked the old man.

'I expect so,' replied the vet. 'And you'll probably win.'

★ Horse maker

A little boy had just returned from a walk in the country with his Granny. 'Mum, Mum,' he called out. 'We've just seen a man who makes horses!'

'Really?' asked his mother.

'Yes, and he'd nearly finished,' said the boy. 'As we walked by he was nailing on its feet.'

★ Bigger than ...

A Texan trainer was visiting Newmarket, and got chatting with an English trainer in a pub. They were discussing the size of training facilities in America versus those in the UK.

'You know, I get on my saddle horse in the morning, and I

could ride him all day long and still not get around the whole of our property,' bragged the Texan.

'Yes,' replied the British trainer. 'I had a horse like that once too.'

★ Hunt balls

A particularly popular Hunt had arranged a formal dinner prior to their annual Hunt Ball, and had asked their local (pro-hunting) MP to make an after-dinner speech. As the MP droned on and on at length, one particular guest who was considerably the worse for drink couldn't stand it any more and lobbed a wine bottle at the MP. Unfortunately, the bottle hit the MFH instead.

'Hit me again,' murmured the MFH as he slumped in his chair, 'I can still hear the so-and-so.'

★ Wrong course

'I've never ridden such a terrible cross-country course in my life,' shouted an irate and muddy competitor to a small group of spectators as she and her horse landed, having awkwardly jumped some hurdles.

'You're half a mile from the course,' one shouted back. 'This is our farmyard.'

★ Excuses

Really annoyed at the employee's request to leave work early for her fourteenth or fifteenth dental appointment that month, the boss complained 'I wish you cared about your work as much as you care about your horses.'

The employee was shocked into honesty. 'No, I could never take work that seriously.'

★ Shipwrecked

A well-known showjumping course builder was shipwrecked and, finding himself washed up on a small desert island, decided to use his time industriously. Eventually his distress signals were picked up by a Navy vessel and a launch was sent out to rescue him. To the amazement of the landing party, when they looked around the island they saw that the castaway had built a crude but excellently planned showjumping course out of driftwood, stones, small shrubs and palm branches.

'Most impressive,' said the officer in charge of the landing party.

'You're very kind, but it's hardly up to my usual standard,' said the rescued course builder.

'However I am rather proud of the water jump...'

★ Terrible twins

A farmer couldn't tell his two horses apart, so he tried cutting one horse's tail several inches shorter than the other's. This worked for a while, until the horse's tail grew out. Then the farmer tried hogging the mane of one horse, which also worked until it grew out. Finally, the farmer found a long-term solution – to measure the horses. And when he did, he discovered that the grey was a full hand taller than the chestnut.

★ Bits and bytes

A trekking trip had been organised in Wales and the leader was getting everybody ready. Several people had never been on a horse before so she said to them, 'It's simple, really. If you want the horse to turn right, pull slightly on the right rein and if you want it to turn left, pull slightly on the left rein. If you pull on both reins the horse will stop, and if you want the horse to move forward or go faster, kick gently.'

At this point a rather studious-looking young tekkie type at the back said, 'Ah, I see. It's a point and kick user interface.'

★ Think shrink

A woman went to see a psychiatrist, very worried about her husband. 'He thinks he's an event horse,' she said. 'He sleeps standing up, whinnies instead of speaking, and even insists on eating hay out of a haynet. It's terrible.'

'How long has this been going on?' asked the psychiatrist.

'Several months now,' replied the woman.

The psychiatrist thought carefully. 'You've let this go too far. Your husband will require lengthy counselling and psycho-analysis which is not available on the National Health, so it will be very expensive.'

'Money doesn't matter, I don't care about the expense,' said the woman. 'I'm prepared to pay whatever it costs to stop my husband thinking he's a horse.'

'But it will be thousands of pounds,' said the psychiatrist. 'Can you really afford all this money?'

'Oh yes,' said the woman. 'He's already won Badminton and Burghley and now he's got full sponsorship from LandRover.'

★ Put-downs

Popular put-downs used by sarcastic riding instructors

'I see you've set aside this special time to humiliate yourself in this manège.'

'I'll try to be nicer if you try to ride better.'

'I like you. You remind me of when I couldn't do a half-pass either.'

'This isn't a manège. This is Hell with sand on the floor.'

'Not all stallions are annoying. Some are dead.'

'I'm trying to imagine you can ride.'

'I would explain the movement to you, but your brain would explode.'

'If I give you a carrot, will you gallop off and leave?'

★ Un-horsed

A cowboy rode into town and stopped at a saloon for a drink. Unfortunately, the locals always had a habit of picking on strangers, which he was. When he finished his drink, he found his horse had been stolen.

He went back into the bar, handily flipped his gun into the air, caught it above his head without even looking and fired a shot into the ceiling.

'Which one of you sidewinders stole my horse!?' he yelled with surprising forcefulness.

No one answered.

'All right, I'm gonna have another beer, and if my horse ain't back outside by the time I finish, I'm gonna do what I dun in Texas! And I don't like to have to do what I dun in Texas!'

Some of the locals shifted restlessly. The man, true to his word, had another beer, walked outside, and his horse has been returned to the post. He mounted up and started to ride out of town.

The bartender wandered out of the bar and asked, 'Say partner, before you go... what happened in Texas?'

The cowboy turned back and said, 'I had to walk home.'

★ Exercises to help you become a better horse person

Drop a heavy object on your foot. Don't pick it up. Shout, 'Get off, you stupid horse! Get off!'

Jump off the back of a LandRover doing around 25 mph. Practise 'relaxing into the fall'. Roll yourself into a ball and then spring up to your feet.

Learn to take your chequebook out of your pocket and write out a cheque for £200 without even looking.

Jog long distances every day, carrying a headcollar and a couple of carrots.

Work on your porkie-telling skills, e.g. 'You see, unloading hay bales is fun, isn't it, darling?' Or 'No, really, I'm glad your good luck and £100,000 dressage horse won you a first in the Medium. I'm just thankful my hard work and real talent won me my second place.'

Practise ringing up your osteopath on your mobile phone with both arms paralysed to the shoulder and one foot anchoring the lead rope of a spooky horse.

Lie face down in the muddiest patch of your field in your best competition riding clothes and brand new leather boots. Repeat several times, 'This is a learning experience, this is a learning experience, this is...etc.'

And the most important exercise of all: marry someone wealthy.

★ Horse sense

A man's car broke down on a country road. While he was peering under the bonnet to see what was wrong, a horse cantered up to the nearby fence and looked over at the car. 'Probably the ignition gone wrong,' said the horse.

The man, startled, ran off down the road until he bumped into a farmer, and told the farmer what had just happened.

'Was it a big black mare with a wide blaze down her face?' asked the farmer.

'Yes, I think so,' said the man.

'Oh, don't listen to her,' said the farmer. 'She doesn't know anything about cars.'

★ Stand-alone

One day at a Pony Club summer camp, a well-known and rather pompous instructor was greeting her pupils.

Having grouped them in a semi-circle facing her, she then stood in the middle and said, 'Would anyone who thinks they're a useless rider please dismount and stand here!'

After a minute or so of silence, one young girl jumped off her pony, handed the reins to the child on the next pony, and stood near the instructor.

'Well, hello. So you actually think you're a useless rider?' the instructor asked.

The girl replied, 'No miss, I just didn't want to see you standing there all by yourself.'

★ Horse advertising jargon demystified

Bold jump Nips over five-bar gate from a standstill when someone tries to catch him.

Home bred Knows nothing other than how to pull up plants in vegetable gardens.

Plenty of bone Good thing it has a mane, tail and little ears, otherwise it would be mistaken for a small elephant.

No vices Especially when wearing muzzle.

Not novice ride Lunatic.

Suit confident teenager Lunatic who likes loud rock music.

Forward going Two paces – standstill and full gallop.

Should make 16hh Dam and sire both 15.2hh but this one might just defy its DNA and grow a bit more.

Well mannered Hasn't stepped on, bitten or kicked anyone for the past week.

No time forces sale Current rider still having daily hospital treatment.

Will make SJ Regularly jumps high fence to get out of paddock.

Will make eventer No brakes.

Will make dressage horse No accelerator.

Will make RC horse No brain.

Quietly brought on Walked about in yard in headcollar, hobbles and muzzle.

Ideal second pony Provided your child is 6 feet tall, weighs 15 stone and is an expert Sumo wrestler.

Fun hack Spooks at crisp packets, carrier bags, birds, lorries, tractors, dogs, etc.

Experienced home only Regularly jumps out of field, gets injured, no manners, bites and kicks.

Schoolmaster Old and decrepit.

Fast against the clock Especially after having dumped rider and is galloping across the showground.

Open to vet Prospective purchaser to pay for current owners to find out, finally, what really is wrong with it.

★ Accidental dressage

During a particularly spectacular pirouette in canter, the horse cast a shoe and it flew over a hedge, down a bank and out of sight. The horse and rider left the manège and went back to the yard, to find their instructor was there waiting to give a lesson to another livery owner. The rider told the instructor about the cast shoe and how it had happened.

'Aha,' said the instructor. 'Do you realise that shoe went over the hedge, down the bank, on to the dual carriageway below, and hit a motorcyclist hard on the head. He went out of control, a lorry and a coach swerved to miss him, collided, rolled over, and by the end of it fourteen vehicles were involved and several people were injured.'

'Oh, my God,' said the rider, by now in tears and extremely distraught. 'What can I do? What can I do?'

The instructor thought carefully for a moment. 'In your shoes, I would use a little more inside leg and shift your weight slightly further round on the outside seat bone.'

★ Life's little realities

Life is an endless struggle full of frustrations and challenges, but eventually you find a farrier who isn't late.

If you can remain calm, you just haven't ridden that course before.

Sometimes I think my horse will go clear in the Open class, then I regain consciousness.

If at first you don't succeed, see how far down the placings the rosettes go.

I had to give up using a synthetic saddle. My thighs kept rubbing on the flaps and setting my jodhpurs on fire.

Amazing! You just hang your black showing jacket in your wardrobe for a while, and it shrinks two sizes.

Freedom of the press means no-iron hunting stocks.

★ Vets' notes on patients' records

'On the second day the hock was better and on the third day it disappeared completely.'

'Clinic discharge status: alive but without permission from owner.'

'Past veterinary history has been remarkably insignificant with only a fifty kilogram weight gain in the past three days.'

'Between you and me, we ought to be able to get this mare in foal.'

'Since we can't get her in foal with AI, I thought you might like to work her up.'

'He is numb from his frogs down.'

'The nostrils were moist and dry.'

'Occasional, constant, infrequent coughing.'

'Colt was alert and unresponsive.'

'Rectal examination revealed a normal size throat.'

'The lab test indicated abnormal lover function.'

'Eyes: Somewhat dull but present.'

'Mare has one healthy foal, but no other abnormalities.'

'Filly was seen in consultation by Mr Blank, who felt we should sit on the tendon and I agree.'

★ Plans for the next Olympic Games

Rugby enthusiasts will recall how the New Zealand All Blacks were motivated by performing 'The Haka' before their world cup games a few years back. Such a custom has now attracted riders from various nations' showjumping teams, and we are privileged to have an early glimpse of what they are planning for the next Olympic Games.

The *England* team will chat about the weather, wave hankies in the air and attach bells to their ankles for a while before moaning about how they were the early stalwarts of the sport, and developed it for the rest of the world, and how it's not fair that everyone can beat them now.

The *Scottish* team will chant 'You lookin' at me Jimmy?' before smashing an Irn Bru bottle over the heads of the other teams' riders.

The *Ireland* team will split into two, with the Southern half performing a Riverdance, while the Northerners march the traditional route from the collecting ring to the main arena via the other teams' stable blocks.

Unfortunately the *Welsh* riders' suggestion has been vetoed by the RSPCA.

Argentina will unexpectedly invade a small part of opposition's stable block, claim it as their own 'Las Box-as' and then be forcibly removed by the British team managers.

Two members of the *South African* team will claim to be more important than the other three whom they will coral in the deepest part of the water jump whilst they claim the rest of the arena for themselves.

The *Americans* will not be there until the jump-off. In future years they will alter the records to show that they were in fact the most important team in the competition and Hollywood will make a film about it called 'Puissance: The Jump That Saved The World'.

Two of the *Canadian* team will sing La Marseillaise and hold the rest of the team to ransom.

The *Italian* team will arrive in flashy red cars, sexually harass the female collecting-ring stewards and then run away.

The *Spanish* will sneak into the other half of the arena, mow it and then claim that it was all in line with the European 'grass quotas'. They will then curl up under the spread fences and have a kip until the jump-off.

The *Japanese* will attempt to strengthen their team by offering good salaries to the key riders in other teams (over 35) and then run around the arena at high speed in a highly efficient manner before buying the whole stadium (with a subsidy from the UK Government).

The *French* will declare they have new scientific evidence that the other teams are in fact all mad. They will then park horseboxes across the middle of the arena, turn their horses out loose into the collecting ring and burn the stewards.

★ How can you tell if you're really a horsey person?

You plan your pregnancy so that the last three months are after the hunting season when the horses are turned away, but so your figure will be back in shape in time for cubbing.

Your teenage daughter proudly tells everyone she's been asked to be a collecting-ring steward at your cousin's wedding.

You hack your horse out for two hours in pouring rain, but won't let your children play football in the garden until the drizzle stops.

Your parents only ever ask you to Sunday lunch in the few weeks around Christmas and New Year, as on any other Sunday they know you're at a dressage competition.

You spend more on your horse's shoes than you do on your own.

When your husband does his own ironing you pat him on the neck and say 'Good boy'.

When looking forward to a 'Happy Event' means your Riding Club team has just qualified for the National Finals.

You get into work in a smart suit and high-heeled shoes, and a colleague discreetly picks some hay out of your hair.

You can never offer people a lift in the back seat of your car unless they're prepared to sit in a bucket full of soaked sugarbeet.

Your children's washing never gets done because the washing machine is always full of cotton girths and numnahs.

When you give directions to someone who is coming to visit you, you say 'Can't miss it, it's the house with the trailers and horsebox in the drive.'

You put your hand in your coat pocket looking for the car keys and pull out a hoofpick.

You forget your mother-in-law's birthday every year, but the horses are always wormed on the dot.

Your father complains about his painful bunions and you recommend remedial farriery.

You shout at your children and kick the cat because your horse refused three times at a brush fence during your lesson.

You run your finger over your children's teeth to see if they need rasping.

You insist that the relocation allowance of any new job you take must include the cost of hiring the lorry to move your horse to his new yard.

The only photographs on your office desk are of your horse, not your husband or children.

The last time you had a lie-in in the morning was when your horse was away being backed.

You won't let your family eat the apples from the tree in your garden, as you're saving them for the horses.

You can only afford to live in rented accommodation but take out a huge bank loan to buy that superb Dutch warmblood.

You pull your horse's mane more often than you go to the hairdresser's.

You put your grandmother's priceless French ormolu clock in the attic to make room on the mantelpiece for your latest Riding Club showjumping trophy.

You take your child to the doctor's with a bad stomach and explain that she was 'off her feed'.

You give your horse a variety of vitamins, minerals and herbal supplements but you still think people get all they need from a normal, balanced diet.

When a rare snowstorm strikes you ring in to work and say you can't get there, but you battle through to the yard in your car to do the horses.

You leave work early with a bad migraine but still manage to get to the yard, muck out and ride for half an hour in the indoor school.

You pay your vet's bill as soon as it arrives, but you wait until the red ones come before you pay for your phone, gas and electricity.

You cheerfully spend two hours a week mucking out your field, but never pick up the dog poos from the lawn in your garden.

You buy a house that's too small, has a leaking roof and needs total renovation, just because it has three loose boxes and six acres of grazing land.

You instinctively push with your inside leg when moving out to the overtaking lane on a motorway.

You half-halt your dog with his lead when out for a walk.

You do the vegetables for supper in the bathroom washbasin because the kitchen sink is full of soaking bits, curb chains and stirrup irons.

You find other people's hair in the shower cubicle offensive, but don't mind the horse hair that finds its way into your clothes via the washing machine.

You look at golf courses and regret their waste of good grazing land.

You say 'Walk on' to your car when the traffic lights change to green.

Your dog jumps a stile awkwardly in a field and you comment that he took off too early.

★ New equine terms

By changing just one or two letters in many well-known words within equine jargon, we can open up a new dimension to our terminology which most horse owners will find useful. For example:

Appaloose Breed of horse known particularly for its fondness for breaking its lead rope when tied to the trailer at shows and galloping about the showground causing chaos.

Brouches Breeches which have inexplicably become painfully tight after having hung unused in your wardrobe for a few years.

Collected banter The pace at which your farrier tells you all the latest gossip from other yards where he works.

Crab biting A condition whereby the horse crib bites sideways.

Crass country A new, politically correct equestrian discipline in which competitors jump obstacles common in urban areas e.g. abandoned stolen cars, stacked supermarket trolleys, dumped milk crates and large, heaped collections of discarded McDonalds cartons.

Dirth A girth which – though long enough in winter months – is inexplicably found to be too short, usually in the late spring when ponies have been stuffing themselves on rich grass.

Dithers The place where the withers should be, but can't be seen or felt, on a fat pony.

Faminitis A disease suffered by many equids, particularly ponies, causing them to escape from their boxes and attempt to raid the feed bins.

Fatlocks Those over-sized plaits you angrily create on the morning of a show, cursing yourself for having forgotten to pull the horse's mane the previous day.

Forelicks The anticipatory slobbering your dogs do while waiting for the farrier's trimmings from your horse's feet.

Gollops The clods of mud flicked into your face by the horse in front while you are all galloping across a damp field.

Heck joint The bony protrusion on a young horse's hind leg that hits you in the chin and causes you to utter an expletive when you're trying to pick his or her hind foot up.

Horsehuge A type of partly fermented forage specially formulated for Shires, Clydesdales, Suffolk Punches,

Percherons, other heavy breeds and heavyweight hunters exceeding 17.2hh.

Hunting stuck A type of neckwear worn by anxious riders who forget the dressage test they should be performing and regret the fact they have not employed the services of a caller.

Lounging Lungeing a lazy horse on a hot sunny day.

Mad fever A personality disorder suffered by horse owners as a result of walking about for prolonged periods in wet, muddy fields chasing after a horse which will not be caught.

Nosebend The shape your nose assumes when your horse has raised its head suddenly in alarm at the same moment that you lean forward.

Poobald A grey horse or pony which has taken a nap in an unskipped-out box after you have bathed him or her ready for a show.

Shoulder-on A dressage movement performed by an owner whose horse has shoved him or her up against the wall of the box while eating and refuses to move out of the way.

Strongles A painful condition of the rider's hands as the result of habitually riding a horse that pulls or leans on the bit.

Sweat itch A condition whereby the horse, having sweated up while being worked, insists on scratching his or her head on the just-dismounted rider's backside.

Thoroughdread A thoroughbred horse who has just noticed a
bin liner that's caught in the hedge and is flapping in the
wind.

Tornout rug A lightweight rug worn by turned-out horses who enjoy picking and eating brambles out of the hedge or reaching for greener grass on the other side of a barbed wire fence.

Warpblood A warmblood with an intense dislike of tractors who has just spotted one coming up the road while out on a hack.

Working haunter The invisible ghost lurking in the bushes behind 'E' in your outdoor manège, that causes your horse to spook nearly every time you pass by it.

★ And some new meanings for existing equine terms

Bog spavin The feeling of panic when riding through marshy areas. Also used to refer to horses who throw a wobbly when asked to go through large puddles.

Colic The gastrointestinal outcome of eating greasy bacon sandwiches from the mobile stands at shows.

Colt What your mare gives birth to when you desperately wanted a filly.

Corn Small growths of hardened skin caused by lengthy wear of cheap leather riding boots.

Endurance ride What happens when your horse spooks and bolts with you through the woods.

Equitation The ability to keep your composure and sit

correctly in the saddle while your horse spooks, shies, bucks and gallops around a show ring.

Fencing Decorative perimeter device designed to provide horses with something to chew, scratch their tails on and jump over.

Grooming The art of brushing the dirt from your horse into your face and on to your clothes.

Grooms Heavy, immovable objects used at shows to hold down folding chairs and to consume the contents of picnic hampers.

Hard feed Costly substance used in the production of large quantities of manure.

Hay Greenish yellow substance that collects in gloves and between layers of clothing, often in quite unspeakable places.

Head shy Reluctance to use the mobile toilets on showgrounds.

Hobbles A horse owner's way of going after having had his/her foot trodden on by his/her horse.

Hoof pick Curved metal instrument that's useful for picking out dried dog poo from the soles of your trainers.

Inbreeding What happens when you postpone the replacement of tired fencing in the field where your yearling colt is turned out.

Jump What a horse does when given an injection or wormer.

Lead rope A long, thick length of plaited twine used to administer rope burns, also used by fizzy horses to take their owner for a drag.

Over-reaching A term used to describe the permanent condition of your credit cards.

Ringworms Spectators who line themselves up six deep by the ropes of show rings and block your view.

Saddle A costly leather or synthetic device designed to give riders a false sense of security – all come with integral ejector mechanisms.

Skip out The action of a horse which stops at a fence, then decides to go around it despite the fact that you're sitting on its ears.

Withers The reason why you rarely see a man riding bareback.

Youngsters A term used to describe horses and ponies old enough to bite and kick, but not yet old enough to chuck you off.

★ Getting carted

A horse-mad young girl had the most awful, near-death experience when she rode this particular horse for the first time. Everything went well for a few moments, but then the horse bolted in full gallop and was totally out of control. She tried desperately to hang on but it was no good, she was sliding off. And worse still, her foot caught in the stirrup iron; she fell headfirst to the ground. Her head bounced harder and harder and still the horse continued to gallop out of control. Just as she was on the point of losing consciousness, the Tesco duty manager walked over and pulled the plug out. What a hero!

★ Heaven knows

One day in Heaven, St Peter, St Paul and St John were standing in the yard, bored. 'Tell you what,' said St Peter. 'Let's put on a showing show. That will give us something interesting to do.'

'Small problem, though,' said St Paul. 'We've got all the best horses here in Heaven. There's no competition.'

'Ah, I have an idea,' said St John. 'Let's invite the Devil to compete. He only has ugly, ill-mannered horses in his yard, so we're bound to win every class.'

The Devil laughed at their idea. 'We would be delighted to compete,' he said, 'and our horses are bound to win every class.'

'Don't be silly,' said St Peter. 'We have all the finest horses here. How could you possibly beat us?'

'Simple,' answered the Devil. 'We've got all the judges.'

★ Posting

A farmer was driving his tractor along a country lane early one morning when he spotted the postman riding his bike towards him. Stopping the tractor, the farmer called out 'Morning! Anything for Mike Howe?'

The postman stopped, searched carefully in his bag and

then looked up at the farmer. "Fraid not, sir,' he said. 'Nothing for your cow, and nothing for your horses either.'

★ Strange tastes

A horse walked into pub at lunchtime and ordered sausage and chips with mustard, ketchup and vinegar. As the horse was eating the landlady stared at him hard.

'I expect you find it strange that a horse should come into your pub and order sausage and chips with mustard, ketchup and vinegar,' said the horse.

'Not at all,' said the landlady. 'That's how I always have my sausage and chips.'

★ How can you tell someone is a farrier?

He changes T-shirts more than four times a day in the summer, but people still hold their noses when he walks into a shop.

He thinks it's normal to come home to messages on the answering machine from women he doesn't know, saying they need him right away.

He watches the way people walk and thinks to himself, 'With the right shoes I could compensate for that.'

He can spend twelve hours a day bent over, but his back aches after standing upright for ten minutes.

Force of habit is such that even when he is dressed up for a night out, he still washes his hands before he goes to the loo as well as afterwards.

If someone is hammering nails on a building site, he will stop and listen carefully.

Despite his not being a lap dancer, his customers still spend more time looking at his backside than at his face.

He thinks working from 8 am to 8 pm is a half day.

He looks ten years younger but feels ten years older than his real age.

★ Ideas for new reasons why the farrier is late

'I got stuck behind the Queen's motorcade and Special Branch wouldn't let me overtake it.'

'My van broke down.' (But never say it's the gearbox. Anyone who has blown a gearbox knows it takes two weeks to have one mended or replaced properly, not two hours. Try shouting at the van and saying 'bloody balljoints'. That always sounds good.)

'I was called out on an emergency case by a vet.' (Always sounds plausible, even though there isn't one vet in the county who will give you the time of day. Make sure you choose the name of a vet who has been dead for a least ten years. That way he or she won't turn up at the yard just as you're telling the customer about it.)

'I'm not late, you got the time wrong.' (Can catch them off guard, but may be a tricky one if you're two days late.)

'I had to go to the dentist's.' (Don't say it was for a check-up. Give a long explanation about the wisdom tooth extraction with plenty of emphasis on blood and pus. The customer will change the subject quickly.)

'My wife got the appointments mixed up.' (Wives are a great source of excuses, but Heaven help you if they ever catch you out. This reason is best avoided if you are single, or a lady farrier.)

'I was kidnapped by aliens.' (Children enjoy this one.)

★ Farriers' reasons for lost shoes

'It was because of the gravitational pull you get when there's a full moon.'

'It was stolen by the poor horses in the next field, as they can't afford one of their own.'

'It got sucked off by mud-consuming alien metal worms.' (Useful if customer is under twelve.)

'Your hoof oil has dissolved it.'

'As I haven't put my prices up for two years I'm forced to use nails made in Taiwan.'

'It's because you're not using magnetic bell boots.'

'Your dog must have been hungry and chewed it off.'

★ Things farriers love to hear from their clients

'Your shoe fell off.'

'He's never kicked anyone else, you must have upset him.'

'It must be a mistake at my bank, try re-presenting it next week.'

'Can you make his foot smaller?'

'*Horse and Rider* magazine says...'

'Everyone at the yard says...'

'Why can't you put the old shoes back on?' (Because you can see light shining through them.)

'He's not really kicking, it's just a nervous twitch.'

★ Names

'I call my horse Carpenter.'

'Why?'

'He's always doing odd jobs around the yard. You should see him make a bolt for an open stable door.'

★ Breeding

A farmer asked his young son to take their Shire mare over to the stallion at the stud farm on the other side of the village. As the little lad was leading the mare along, they met the Vicar.

'Where are you going?' asked the Vicar, concerned that such a small boy was in charge of such a large horse.

'I'm taking the mare to the stallion, Vicar,' said the boy.

'Couldn't your father do it? Or can I help?'

'No, sorry, Vicar. It has to be the stallion.'

★ Hot dinners

The local Riding Club arranged a Christmas dinner for its large committee, but unfortunately the event was not up to much. One committee member complained to the Club Secretary.

'The food was awful,' he said. 'Can you do something about it?'

'No,' replied the Secretary. 'You'll just have to bring it up at the next committee meeting.'

★ Doctor

A young woman went to the doctor with a badly sprained ankle. The doctor strapped it up for her.

'Will I be able to ride a horse when it's better?' she asked.

'Of course you will,' replied the doctor.

'That's funny,' said the woman. 'I've never ridden a horse in my life before.'

★ Muddles

A middle-aged horsewoman ran into her childhood riding instructor who was by now very old. 'Ah yes,' said the old instructor. 'I remember, your name is Simpson.'

'That's right,' said the former pupil. 'How clever of you to recognise me after all those years!'

'Tell me,' continued the old instructor, 'was it you or your sister who got killed in that dreadful hunting accident?'

★ Eyeballs

A well-known eventing team coach had lost an eye as the result of a bad fall at Badminton, and had been fitted with a false one. It was so lifelike that one of his pupils asked his assistant how she knew it was a false eye.

'Oh,' she replied, 'He and I were chatting one day and it just came out in the conversation.'

★ Steps

A stud farm manager had taken on a work experience pupil and decided to teach her a few things about how to handle horses.

'Now just suppose you walked up to that field and realised the gate had been left open. You can see twenty mares galloping right at you and the busy road beyond. What steps would you take?'

The girl thought for a moment. 'Very long and fast ones, Mr Davis.'

★ Timing

The elderly, retired MFH ran into his old Whipper-In at the Hunt Ball. 'Good to see you again, Jackson,' said the old Master. 'How are things with you?'

'Not so good, sir, if I'm honest,' replied the Whipper-In. 'In fact I haven't had a decent day's hunting since 1955.'

The Master looked at his watch. 'My, that was quick work,' he said. 'It's only 20:30 now.'

★ Sick leave

A distinctly unpopular Riding Club chairperson was taken ill and had to spend two weeks in hospital. While there, she received a Get Well card from the RC committee. Under the signature someone had written 'The decision to send this card was carried by seven votes to six.'

★ Little boy lost

A little boy was found wandering about on a showground, obviously lost, so someone took him to the Secretary's tent to see if his mother could be found.

The Secretary smiled kindly at the little boy and said, 'I'm sure we'll find your Mummy. What's she like?'

The little boy thought for a moment. 'Trakehners and Andalusians.'

★ Time fault

An irate competitor looked up at the judges' box in an indoor showjumping arena after she had completed a perfect clear round with just one time fault.

'What would you do if I said you're a bunch of pernickety old fools?' she shouted.

'We would disqualify you,' came the reply.

'All right,' continued the competitor. 'Suppose I just thought that you were?'

'Well,' came the voice on the PA, 'there's nothing much we could do about that.'

'Good,' shouted the competitor as she walked her horse out of the arena. 'I think you're a bunch of pernickety old fools.'

★ Dislocation

An event rider had a crashing fall on the cross-country course and dislocated his shoulder. He was taken to the Accident and Emergency unit at the nearest hospital, where the medics attempted to put his shoulder back into place without an anaesthetic. The rider shouted and screamed in agony.

'Listen, just try to be brave, ok?' said a junior doctor. 'There's a woman having a baby in the next cubicle and she's not making half the noise you are.'

'Maybe not,' screamed the rider. 'But they're not trying to put it back!'

★ Fishy

An angler was fishing by the river bank, when he suddenly saw a helmet floating by, going against the current. 'Are you all right?' he shouted.

A hand came up out of the water and waved. 'Yes, thanks,' came the reply. 'I'm on a horse.'

★ Boots

A man bought a pair of riding boots that were two sizes too small for him. When someone asked him why, he said 'My wife has left me, my livery yard has gone bankrupt, and my own horse has gone lame. Now the only pleasure I have left in life is when I take my boots off at the end of the day.'

★ Riding for a fall

The Head Girl in the riding school yard was furious as one of the working pupils arrived late again. 'Angela,' she yelled, 'you should have been here at half-past seven!'

'Why?' asked the pupil. 'What happened?'

★ Who's racing?

Three stable lads at a racing yard were always playing cards when the Head Lad wasn't around. One day he was tiptoeing by and saw them, so he thought he would give them a fright to teach them a lesson. He rang the fire alarm bell three times, then waited to watch their reaction. To his amazement, nothing happened. Then, a couple of minutes later, the barman from the pub across the road arrived in the yard with three pints of beer.

★ Driving troubles

A young pupil was very proud that one of our most famous carriage driving champions was coming to her yard to give her a private lesson. She stayed up all the previous night cleaning the harness, the pony and the cart. Finally the moment came when they set off in the cart with everything looking fantastic. They were going along splendidly when suddenly the pony rather noisily broke wind.

'Oh gosh, I am sorry about that,' said the young pupil.

'No problem,' smiled the famous champion. 'If you hadn't said anything I would have thought it was the pony.'

★ Heaven again

An old Portuguese dressage master who was known for his terrible temper and rude language died and went to Heaven. St Peter greeted him politely at the Pearly Gates and in a friendly way, asked him to supply his name. In a gruff voice, the dressage master told him.

'Well,' said St Peter, 'you can come in, provided you don't shout at God when He can't get His horse into an outline.'

★ Livery fee

The yard manager walked over to one of the livery owners as she was grooming her horse. 'I'm sorry, but I'm going to raise your weekly livery fee.'

The owner smiled and said, 'Thank Heaven for that. Now I won't have to do it every week.'

★ More boots

A horse had received a light kick on the cannon bone – nothing serious, just a little bruising. The owner went into the local chemist's to buy some Witch Hazel to apply to the bruised area.

'Sorry,' said the pharmacist, 'we're out of Witch Hazel at the moment. Why don't you try Boots?'

'Well,' replied the owner, 'they might be ok for a tendon injury but this is just some mild bruising.'

★ Ring, ring

A well-known breeder of Welsh Cobs was sitting quietly reading his paper when his wife sneaked up behind him and whacked him on the head with a frying pan.

'What was that for?' he said.

'That was for the piece of paper in your trouser pocket with the name Blodwyn written on it,' she replied.

'Don't be silly,' he said, smiling. 'Last week when I went to the auctions that was the name of a mare I wanted to bid on.'

She looked satisfied, apologised, and went off to carry on with getting supper. Three days later he was sitting in his chair once more, reading the paper, when she whacked him with an even bigger frying pan, knocking him out. When he came round, he said, 'What the hell was that for?'

'That mare rang up and asked to speak to you.'

★ Baby's nose

A National Hunt jockey was in bed with his wife, reading his copy of *Horse & Hound*. He glanced up and looked at the couple's baby, who had a slight cold. She was in her cot by the bed.

'Baby's nose is running again,' he commented, returning to *Horse & Hound*.

His wife snorted. 'That's all you ever think about – racing!'

★ Very cross country

A competitor in a horse trial had completely lost her way and couldn't fathom where the course went from the previous fence. She trotted her horse up and down for several minutes, ranting and raving. After a little longer a kindly old lady, who was sitting watching with her family, shouted out to the competitor, 'Would I be breaking the rules if I told you where the next fence is?'

★ Trophies

A woman had been a member of a Riding Club for many years but despite competing regularly had never won anything. One day she bumped into the Club Secretary in Tesco and announced that she had just given birth to triplets. At a Club committee meeting that night, the Secretary suggested they present this member with a special prize for the birth of the triplets, as she had never won anything before. They agreed. Two weeks later at the Club's AGM, the member was awarded with a silver cup. When the delighted woman accepted it, she suddenly looked concerned. 'Is this a one-off trophy, or is it to be an annual Challenge Cup?'

★ Doctor

A middle-aged rider came home from a visit to the Doctor's. 'The doctor said I should give up dressage,' he moaned to his wife.

'Why – did she examine your heart?' asked the wife.

'No,' said the man. 'She took a look at my score sheets.'

★ Hospital visit

An elderly livery yard owner was taken ill and rushed to
hospital. At one point the medical staff thought she might die,
so summoned everyone to the hospital. The yard owner's
eyelids flickered as she asked who was there, and all her
family and staff from the yard called out to say yes, they were.
The yard owner suddenly sat bolt upright in bed and shouted,
'You're all here? Then who the hell is doing the horses this
morning?'

★ Professional fees

A vet had been invited to an important Chamber of
Commerce dinner in the town and was held up during the
pre-dinner drinks by a woman who button-holed him at
length, asking questions about her horse's tendon problems.
When the vet eventually reached the dinner table he found he
was sitting next to a solicitor, to whom he complained about
the woman.

'Do you think I should send her a bill?' asked the vet.

'Of course you should,' smiled the solicitor. 'You were
delivering veterinary consultation.'

The next day when the vet opened his post at the surgery,
he found a letter from the solicitor accompanied by an invoice
'To legal consultation, £50.'

★ Nobel prize

A man stopped by his friend's yard one evening to say hello.
He noticed that his friend's car was parked there, the horses
were all in, rugged up in their Thermatexes and munching at

their haynets, the feeds were made up for the next morning, but his friend was nowhere to be found. Eventually, the man decided to have a look in the field, in case there had been an accident. To his amazement his friend was out in the middle of it, just standing there.

'What on earth are you doing out there?' the man shouted to his friend.

'Trying to win a Nobel Prize,' the friend shouted back.

'How are you going to do that?' called the man, in astonishment.

'Well,' his friend called back, 'I've heard they give the Nobel Prize to people who are out standing in their field.'

★ Compensation

A rather eccentric elderly horse owner was approached by the railway authorities who were planning a new rail route through one of his fields. They offered him a huge sum of money in compensation for the land amounting to twenty times its real value, but he turned it down.

'Why on earth did you do that?' asked a friend. 'That field's full of ragwort and the money would keep your horses for years.'

'That's as may be,' said the horse owner. 'But I'm too old to go out there and open the ruddy gate every time a train's coming through.'

★ Foreign climes

In darkest Arabia, a sheikh needed to make a journey across the desert. He didn't have a horse to hand so he decided to expropriate one from a nearby group of Nomads. Two suitable horses were found, but neither of the owners wanted to give theirs up and each said his horse was useless. 'Right,' said the sheikh, 'you will race your horses, and I will have the winner.'

'All they'll do is hold their horses back,' pointed out one of the sheikh's entourage.

'No they won't,' replied the sheikh. 'Get each man to ride the other one's horse.'

★ Coming or going

A true townie decided it might be fun to go on a pony-trekking holiday in the Lake District, so set off with jaunty confidence despite the fact that he had never ridden before and knew nothing about horses. After a basic lecture on the first afternoon, the next morning he was cheerfully tacking up his pony when the Head Girl stopped and said, 'You do realise, don't you, that you're putting the saddle on back to front?'

'Aha,' replied the cheeky townie. 'But you don't know which way I'm going to go.'

★ Hiccups

A keen showjumping rider had made entries for a full season of competitions and was working very hard for it, schooling the horses and training every day, all hours of the day and night. Suddenly she developed a bad case of hiccups and despite trying every home cure, nothing worked, so she went to the doctor.

After examining her carefully the doctor said, 'I'll tell you what your problem is. You're pregnant.'

She fell into a chair, clutching her brow. 'Oh no, what a

terrible shock! I've got competitions every weekend for the next six months! Surely it can't be true?' she shouted.

'No, it's not true,' said the doctor. 'But it certainly has cured your hiccups.'

★ Tick, tick

'I still don't know what makes the Head Girl tick,' said the working pupil at the riding school. 'But I do know what makes her explode.'

★ Feet first

A young apprentice had just started work for the local farrier. On his first morning he was amazed when the farrier said, 'No, no, put those tools away. The first thing you have to learn is to look at the horse's feet, then stand up straight and say "What did the last farrier use, then? Paper clips?"'

★ Pay rise

The stable lad got his courage together and went to see the yard manager to ask for a rise. When he entered the office, the yard's accountant was there too. 'I'd like a pay rise,' stammered the young stable lad.

'Well, young man,' said the accountant while the yard manager nodded wisely, 'due to the fluctuational predisposition of the global competitive equestrian economic climate as juxtaposed against the individual staff productivity within this particular enterprise, in my judgement I feel it would be fiscally inappropriate to elevate exponentially your specific increment.'

'Yer what?' said the puzzled stable lad. 'I don't get it.'

'Exactly,' said the yard manager.

★ How many horses does it take to change a light bulb?

Warmblood Light bulb? What light bulb?

Thoroughbred Oh no, not a light bulb gone! How terrifying! Why do you have to scare me like that!

Dales Just me of course, and I'll rewire the stable block at the same time.

New Forest Light bulb? Light bulb? That thing I just ate was a light bulb?

Suffolk Punch You didn't eat it. I breathed on it and it broke.

Hanoverian How DARE that light bulb go! How DARE you ask me to change it! OH! (flounces off)

Welsh Cob Don't change it. If it's dark no one will see me raid the feed bins.

Dartmoor None. Dartmoors aren't afraid of the dark.

Arab That's what we pay you for. And I'll chew on your jacket while you do it.

Lusitano Let the housekeeper do it. I'm off to roll in the mud.

Show Pony Lights? Lights? Where? Do you want me straight on, or in profile? This is my good side, no wait, my mane's not plaited, oh couldn't you pick a better time?

Shire (yawning) Who gives a monkeys?

Irish Draught There's no way I'm doing anything until I've finished my haynet. Can't you see I'm busy?

Selle Français Zut alors, somebody go ring ze electrician.

Shetland I can't reach the stupid light.

★ Amateur dramatics

A rather green but very wealthy racing enthusiast was thrilled
when he heard that Jimmy Riddle, a big winner over the
sticks that season, had come up for sale. 'That's great news
for me as I've always wanted to own a racehorse,' he said to
the owner, 'but why do you want to sell him when he's doing
so well?'

'Oh,' said the horse's owner, 'I'm fed up with him. He's so
vain, and such an actor! Last time out he was winning by
several lengths and would you believe, he slowed down to a
canter at the end just so he'd be on camera for a photo finish!
And he even made sure his head was turned just the right
way so the camera would get his best profile!'

'I don't care if he's Sean Connery,' said the racing
enthusiast, 'I'll take him.'

They went up to Jimmy Riddle's box and the owner put on
his headcollar, ready to lead him out into the yard. 'Okay,
Jimmy,' the owner said loudly. 'Now show this nice man your
best impression of a lame horse.'

★ Responsibility

The manager of showjumping yard telephoned the manager
of another, similar yard some fifty miles away and shouted
angrily, 'In your reference for this groom, you said she was a
responsible worker!'

'She is,' came the reply. 'In the time she was here seven
horses got colic, fourteen got thrush, the tack room got
ransacked, rats got into the feed stores and I nearly had a
nervous breakdown. And in each case, she was responsible.'

★ A real dressage test

A: Enter in working trot, jerky serpentine

X: Halt

G: Try to halt again

C: Freeze in horror at judge's ferocious glare. Salute hurriedly

C: Track left

H: Working rustle of spectator's crisp packet

HXF: Extended bolt

F: Track right (just)

FAKE: Working gallop right

E: Circle right 20 metre strange polyhedron

E: Freestyle pirouette, change rein

EKAFB: Counter canter, cross canter, camel canter

B: Medium bird shuffling in bush

BX: Working spook left

X: Freestyle piaffe

XK: Freestyle half-pass (backwards)

KEHCMBFA: Working trot (bouncing)

A: Turn right

ADXG: Extended walk

G: Halt. Attempted immobility. Trembling salute.
   Leave arena at walk on long rein, muttering
   'You're dogmeat now' under breath.

★ Exchange

'Last week I got a lovely Welsh Cob for my husband.'
   'I've seen your husband. That sounds like a reasonable
swap.'

★ Names

What do you call a man who, while his partner does the horses, cooks breakfast and takes the kids to school, spends all weekend mucking out the fields and stacking bales, drives the lorry so she can relax on the way to and from shows, and earns enough to buy her that superb Trakehner she's always fancied?

Darling.

★ Poets' corner

Ode to motorists in country lanes

Some motorists are very kind
To horses somewhat heated
You slow and stop, with engines off,
So we can remain seated.

The trouble is once we have gone
Beyond your line of vision
You fire your engine, roaring loud
With racing-start precision.

Creating thus some equine fear
Your clutch engages, wallop!
Your tyres bite on verge and grit
Then horse goes into gallop.

And lorry drivers, you're the best
At seeing us fast departed.
If when we're feet from a lorry's rear
Your airbrakes have just f*rted.

So though we're grateful for the thought
From all you careful drivers
Please wait till we are truly past
Or you'll need to revive us.

★ Nursery rhymes

Hickory dickory dock
Jump off against the clock
The horse struck one
Four faults were done
'Oh, Hickory dickory ... damn!'

Ring a ring o' roses
Is where my pony's nose is
A-tishoo, a-tishoo
That'll teach him to nibble at hedges out on a hack.

Little Miss Maddle
Sat in the saddle
Eating her Burger King
When came a bike rider
That revved up beside her
And her horse began fast galloping.

Poor Little Miss Maddle
Fell out of the saddle
Straight on to her safety hat
Still clutching her burger
Her shouts threatened murder
'Now I can't have my french fries with that!'

Jack and Jill went up the hill
To try to jump the water
Jack made a hash and fell with a splash
But Jill jumped clear as one oughta.

Mary had a little horse
Which kicked like there's no tomorrow
And everywhere that Mary went
No other horse dared follow.

Three stroppy mares
Three stroppy mares
See how they bite
See how they bite
They all ran after the farrier
And bit him on his posterior
It made him feel so inferior
Three stroppy mares.

Mary Mary quite contrary
How did the dressage test go?
Counter-canter went well but my half-pass was hell
So in all it was quite a poor show.

Little Bo-Porse got bucked off her horse
And she's no idea where to find him
Leave him alone, he'll make his way home
Trailing his reins behind him.

Oats, chaff, maize and sugarbeet go
Oats, chaff, maize and sugarbeet go
Can you or I or anyone know
How that pony keeps raiding the feed bins, ho-ho?

Little Boy Blue, don't blow your horn
My horse is so fizzy
He's being fed on corn
What would occur if you blew it, d'you think?
We'd be in the next county before you could blink.

Neigh, neigh, racehorse
Have you got a brain?
No sir, no sir
Just a fancy name.
I spook at the master
I spook at the dame
I spook at nearly everything I see down the lane.

Old MacDonald had a yard
Ee i ee i oh
And on that yard he had some livery owners
Ee I ee I oh
With a gossip-gossip here
And a gossip-gossip there
Scandal, intrigue everywhere
Old MacDonald had a yard
Ee I ee I oh.

★ Horses' New Year resolutions

1. I will not spend my spare time thinking up new ways to undo the bottom bolt on my box door.

2. I will not, repeat not, spook at those two evil German Shepherds who airmail themselves at the gate across the road each time we go by.

3. I will chew the paddock fence evenly, not work on the second rail on the left every day until I've bitten right through it.

4. I will not lay my ears back at that loud, patronising instructor even though she calls me a stubborn old mule and taps me on the private parts with her schooling whip.

5. I will be patient with that snotty little Exmoor even though he chases me around the field like a collie rounding up sheep.

6. I will be nice to the farrier even when he slaps my bottom with a left hook like Mike Tyson's and shouts at me in a voice that makes a foghorn sound subtle.

7. I will always remember to dung in the same corner of my box so it doesn't take an hour to skip out every day.

8. I will never, ever chew a human's Barbour again no matter how strong a smell of Polo mints is wafting up from the pockets.

9. I will never try to snatch some young leaves from a hedge while out on hack, no matter how appetising they look.

10. I will not rub the top of my tail on the old apple tree in the paddock so it will never look like a dead hedgehog again.

★ Enjoy, bitte

A well-known British event rider was invited to give a lecture to a group of budding young eventers in Germany. When members of the audience were finishing off their pre-session coffee her German host came up to her and said, 'Vould you like to give your lecture now, or shall ve let ze audience enjoy zemselves for a bit longer?'

★ Lectures again

A famous dressage master, known for his rather pompous and boring way of teaching, delivered a lecture to a Riding Club group on the finer points of haute école. Although very learned and worthy, the lecture went on and on for nearly three hours and without any visual aids or demonstrations to liven it up, had all but sent everyone to sleep. When he finally sat down and the audience applauded politely, he smiled haughtily at the Riding Club Chairman and said, 'Well, Mrs Simpson, now how would you have delivered that lecture?'

The Chairman smiled back at him and said, 'Probably under an assumed name.'

★ Pheasants

Two pony breeders in Wales had a major dispute over land ownership and eventually the whole thing went to County Court. George, one of the breeders, was a wily old fellow and everyone in the local valleys knew that he had been the transgressor, but his solicitor was amazed when he won the case. When he asked George why he thought the judge had found in his favour, George said, 'Simple, boyo. I sent the judge a brace of pheasant.' The solicitor was horrified, of course, and said he could have been done for attempted bribery as well as losing the case. George just smiled and said, 'Ah, yes, but I sent them in the other breeder's name.'

★ Smoking

An incredibly wealthy foreign racing stable owner was known to have a particular dislike of cigarette smoking. One day he was in the UK, touring his magnificent yard near Newmarket and caught a young lad smoking in the tackroom.
Immediately the owner pointed out that the penalty for smoking was instant dismissal, and asked the lad how much he earned. The lad quickly said £200 a week.

The owner fished £800 in cash out of his pocket, thrust it into the lad's hand and said, 'Right, there's a month's wages, you're sacked.' The young lad took the money and left. It was only much later that the owner discovered the lad was a delivery boy who worked for their saddlery supplier, and had been waiting in the tackroom while the yard manager checked through the order of twenty pairs of reins.

★ Bang

An elderly country gentleman had ridden to hounds until he was nearly ninety. He attributed his long life and good health to his rather unusual habit of a daily dose of gun powder. When he finally died aged 97, he left six children, fourteen grand-children and a 48-foot crater at the crematorium.

★ Optimism

Probably the best example of optimism was the man who got married for the first time aged 92, and bought a house with stabling and paddocks in case the children would want to keep ponies.

★ Horse dealer

A little boy and his mother were walking through a cemetery one afternoon and the little boy stopped to look at the epitaph on a headstone. It said, 'Here lies a horse dealer and an honest man.' The little boy read it carefully then turned to his mother and said, 'Mummy, why did they bury two people in the same grave?'

★ Fall out

Two friends had entered a carriage driving competition, as driver and groom, with a team of four horses. As they negotiated the obstacles at full gallop, the groom began to get a little nervous. He shouted to his friend, 'If the carriage turns over, do you think we'll fall out?'

'No, don't be silly,' his friend shouted back. 'After all, we've been friends for twenty years.'

★ That's entertainment

A breeder was taking a lorry load of Shetland ponies to a horse show. Just a few miles from the showground her lorry broke down, so she hailed a passing cattle lorry which fortunately was empty, and said to the driver she'd give him £100 if he'd take the ponies to the show. The lorry driver loaded them up and went off, and the breeder started the long wait for breakdown service to turn up. About an hour later she was amazed to see the cattle lorry come back and stop beside her, the ponies still all loaded up in the back. She shouted out 'But I gave you £100 to take them to the show!' The driver shouted back 'Oh, but the tickets only came to £50. So I'll take them to the pictures now.'

★ Three's a crowd

A faithful old groom had worked for a horse dealer for twenty-five years before he finally plucked up courage to ask for a pay rise. When he did, the dealer said, 'Sam, business is bad right now. I can't afford it.' The poor chap turned round and said 'But I'm doing the work of three grooms!' The boss was furious and said, 'Three grooms' work? Tell me their names, and I'll sack them.'

★ Carry on

The local veterinary practice had a client who ran a showjumping yard, and who was notoriously slow in settling his bills. In the end they got so fed up with him that the senior partner wrote to him personally, saying 'Considering that we've done more for you than your mother did, we would be grateful if you would settle your account immediately.' The yard owner rang up a couple of days later and said, 'What do you mean, you did more for me than my mother did?' 'Well,' replied the senior vet, 'according to our computer we've been carrying you for the last fifteen months.'

★ Wakey wakey

A meteorically successful American showjumper said her definition of real success is, when you jump out of bed at 5 am every day and shout 'Great, another day' ... and then you can afford to go back to bed because someone else is doing the horses.

★ Lorries

An up-and-coming dressage rider decided that she could
finally afford a lorry after years of dragging a trailer around.
She went to see a suitable specimen and asked to go out for a
test drive in it. After they'd been round the block the dealer
looked over at her and said, 'I think honestly you could say
that this lorry is the opportunity of a lifetime.' And the
dressage rider said, 'Yes, I can hear it knocking.' But the
dealer was indignant and said, 'We stand behind every lorry
we sell.' So the dressage rider said, 'Yes, but are you prepared
to push it as well?'

★ Broken down

A famous showjumping trainer was asked to give a lecture at
an annual Instructors' Conference. He asked the Chairman to
give him some details about the instructors in the audience.
'You know,' he said, 'numbers, broken down by age and sex.'
And the Chairman replied, 'Yes, they are.'

★ Wrong number

It was in the early hours of the morning and the mare was
foaling. The owner, fearing a less than uncomplicated
delivery, rang the vets' emergency call-out number on her
mobile phone only to find it was answered by a locum vet she
had never spoken to before. 'My mare is foaling and I think
something's going wrong,' shouted the owner down the
phone.
   'Is this her first foal?' asked the vet.
   'No, you idiot!' screamed the owner. 'This is her owner!'

★ Rude words

A little boy was hauled up in front of the Headteacher for swearing in class. 'We really can't tolerate a pupil using language like that, Thomas,' said the Head. 'Wherever did you hear it?'

'Mummy says it,' replied the boy.

'Surely not,' said the Head. 'Anyway, you don't even know what it means.'

'Yes I do,' piped up the little boy. 'It means the horse is standing on my foot.'

★ Heavens above

A woman who was a very keen dressage rider went on holiday to Rome and by sheer luck managed to secure a private audience with the Pope. 'Your Holiness,' she asked humbly, 'I am a very keen dressage rider and have always wanted to know if there are good dressage horses and competitions in Heaven?'

The Pope thought for a moment and replied, 'I do not know, my good woman, but I will speak to God. Return at the same time tomorrow and I will tell you.'

The woman came back the next day, eagerly awaiting his Holiness's reply. As she stood before him, he smiled and said, 'My good woman, I have good news and bad news relating to your question. The good news is that in Heaven there are as many horses as you could wish for, all trained up to Grand Prix level; there is a beautiful full-sized indoor arena with a superb surface, and there are competitions being held every day.'

'Oh, that's wonderful, your Holiness!' exclaimed the woman. 'But what is the bad news?'

The Pope's smile faded. 'The bad news is, your time for the Novice 27 test is 9:43 tomorrow morning.'

★ That's business

The very wealthy owner of a huge bloodstock stud welcomed his new son-in-law into the family. 'Jeremy,' he said, 'to show how much I love my daughter and value you as her husband, I have just made you a 50-50 partner in the stud business. All you have to do is to come in every day and learn about horses and breeding.'

'But I can't stand horses,' said the son-in-law. 'They bite and kick. And they smell.'

'Very well,' said the father-in-law. 'You can work in the stud office and manage the administration.'

'I hate office work,' replied the son-in-law. 'I can't stand being stuck behind a desk all day.'

'Wait a minute,' said the father-in-law. 'I just made you a half-owner of a profitable stud, but you don't like horses and won't work in a office. What am I going to do with you?'

'Easy,' said the son-in-law. 'Buy me out.'

★ Politically correct equine terms

In our current climate of avoiding potential offence and involuntary discrimination against any creature which faces more than its fair share of daily challenges, CREEOPS (Campaign for Reinforcing Equal Equine Opportunities) has decreed that these former equine terms be replaced as shown overleaf:

Old term: a horse that...	Is ... politically correct term
Wind sucks	Respiratorily over-active
Weaves	Horizontally compulsive
Bolts	Speed-obsessive
Rears	Vertically mobile
Bucks	Ejectorily mobile

Bites	Dentally hyper-active
Raids the feed bins	Gastronomically driven
Persistently refuses	Levitationally challenged
Spooks	Imaginatively alarmist
Leans on the bit	Forehandedly unbalanced

★ What's in a name

A horse dealer and his wife were driving around Wales in their lorry, looking for bargain ponies to bring back to England to sell. At one point they entered a small town with a typically Welsh name, consisting of numerous consonants and few vowels. They began to argue over how it should be pronounced, but couldn't agree. After a few minutes they decided to stop for something to eat and a coffee. As the waitress brought their orders to the table, the horse dealer said to her, 'My wife and I can't agree over how to pronounce the name of this place. Could you please tell us how it should be pronounced?'

The waitress put her tray down and said very slowly, 'L.i.t.t.l.e ...C.h.e.f'.

★ Quick ring

(On telephone) 'Hello, is that the local riding school?'

'Depends where you're ringing from.'

★ Genie's lamp

A woman was out on a hack one day when she spotted a Genie's lamp. She jumped off her horse, picked up the lamp and rubbed it, and lo-and-behold a Genie appeared. The amazed woman asked if she got three wishes.

The Genie said, 'No, due to government cutbacks, the high value of the dollar against the Euro and fierce global competition, I can only grant you one wish. So...what'll it be?'

The woman didn't hesitate. She pulled out a document from her jacket pocket and said, 'I want peace in Eastern

Europe and the Baltics. See this map? I want these countries to stop fighting with each other.'

The Genie looked at the map and exclaimed, 'Come off it, duck! These countries have been at war for thousands of years. I'm good, but not that good! I don't think it can be done. Make another wish.'

The woman thought for a minute and said, 'Well, I've never been able to find a farrier who wasn't late. The hours I spend every year waiting for the farrier, when I could be putting my time to far better use ... yes, that's what I wish for. A good farrier who is always on time.'

The Genie let out a long sigh and said, 'Let's have another look at that map.'

★ In foal

A woman was out for a hack on her large, very fat gelding and when he obstinately refused to move over to the side of the road to make way for a car, she tapped him on the quarters with her whip. As the car drove past a very self-righteous passenger stuck his head out of the window and shouted, 'It's disgusting! Beating that poor mare when she is so obviously pregnant!'

Horse and rider had stopped by this time, and as the car pulled up a few feet away the gelding decided to use the opportunity to urinate. A witty local person who knew the equine pair, and who had heard the man shout indignantly, strode up to the car window and said, 'Shockin', ain't it? Now her waters have broken and there's a leg sticking out.'

★ Elementary, my dear...

Sherlock Holmes and Dr Watson went on a riding holiday in the West Country. After a good meal and a bottle of wine around the campfire, having ensured their horses were safe and secure, they lay down for the night and went to sleep.

Some hours later, Holmes awoke and nudged his companion. 'Watson, raise your eyes and tell me what you observe.'

Watson replied, 'I observe millions of stars.'

'What does that indicate to you?'

Watson thought for a moment. 'Astronomically, it indicates that there are millions of galaxies and probably billions of planets. Astrologically, I observe that Pluto is in Pisces. Horologically, I estimate that the time is approximately 04.00 hours. Theologically, I feel that God is all powerful and that we are tiny and insignificant. Meteorologically, I predict that we will enjoy a fine day tomorrow. Why, what does it indicate to you?'

Holmes was speechless for a moment, then spoke. 'Watson, you idiot. Some so-and-so has stolen our tent.'

★ Jumps

The day before a regional showjumping competition the Show Secretary was frantic, sorting paperwork and taking phone calls. At one point she took a call from a man who asked, 'Am I right in thinking your jumps tomorrow will be from 4,000 feet?'

'No, only up to 3'9" in the Open Class,' she replied absent-mindedly.

'Oh,' said the man. 'Either I'm going to have a very boring day or this is the wrong number for the Parachute Club.'

★ Rear lights

A man and his wife were driving back from a distant showjumping competition late one night, when a police car pulled them over to the side of the road. The officer approached the driver, who rolled down his window.

'Are you aware that you're driving without rear lights, sir?' asked the officer.

With that, the driver flung open his door and ran around to the rear of the car, groaning and clutching his forehead. He was so upset that the officer took pity on him, and said kindly, 'It's not exactly a hanging offence, sir. In fact it really isn't serious.'

'Of course, it's serious!' cried the man. 'I've lost my trailer with the horse inside it!'

★ Wee problem

A private school had arranged a wonderful excursion for its younger pupils in the 2nd, 3rd and 4th forms – a trip to a local point-to-point race meeting. The children were accompanied by two female teachers. After enjoying their lunchtime picnic, the teachers reckoned that the children should visit the portable toilets before the races began. It was decided that the girls would go with one teacher, and the boys with the other.

The teacher assigned to the boys thought it better to remain outside while they did their business. However, after a couple of minutes one of the 3rd-form boys came out and told her that none of them could reach the urinals.

Deciding that her duty to the pupils should over-ride modesty, the teacher went into the gents toilet area and began lifting each boy up, her arms hoisting them under their armpits. She worked her way down the line and when she reached one particular boy, she couldn't help but notice that he was, shall we say, very mature for his age.

'You must be in the 4th,' she commented to him, trying hard not to stare.

'No, I'm in the 6th riding Masterson Shadow, actually,' he replied. 'But thanks for the lift.'

★ Stripes

An elderly female zebra had delighted visitors at the zoo for many years, so when she fell due for retirement the zoo keeper arranged for her to go to his friend's 'open farm' where she could be spoiled and pampered throughout her last days.

The zebra had never seen domestic animals before, so when she arrived at the farm she decided to find out what all these interesting new species were and what they did. The first creature she approached was small and furry with long ears. 'What are you, and what do you do?' asked the zebra.

'I'm a rabbit,' replied the creature, 'and the children love to cuddle me.'

Next she approached a larger creature with curved horns. 'What are you, and what do you do?' she asked.

'I'm a goat, and the children like to stroke me,' answered the goat.

Then, the zebra spotted a much larger creature in the adjacent paddock. It was very like her, a little larger, but with a gleaming chestnut coat, a long, flowing mane and a carefully groomed tail, which she carried at a high angle. 'My goodness, what are you, and what do you do?' asked the zebra.

'I'm an Arab mare, and I just stroll elegantly around the

paddock so everyone can admire me,' replied the mare.

'Well, if you're a horse, we're related,' said the zebra. 'May I come and live with you in your paddock?'

The Arab mare looked down her beautiful dished face at the zebra. 'Well, I suppose so,' she said reluctantly, 'but you'll have to change out of those AWFUL pyjamas first.'

★ One-uphorsemanship

A huge, air-conditioned horsebox had encountered a red traffic light and was waiting for it to change when a tatty old LandRover pulling a worn-out double horse trailer also pulled up. The snooty dressage rider in the passenger seat of the smart lorry buzzed the electric window down and began boasting to the driver of the LandRover that hers was the best horse transport money could buy.

'This lorry has ABS, airbags for all passengers and for the horses as well, automatic climate control, onboard computer control system, photochromic glass, five-star accommodation including water beds for the grooms, a mini-bar, a television with satellite dish embedded in the roof ....'

At this point the LandRover and trailer driver interrupted.

'But do you have internet access in there?'

The light changed at this point, and the lorry pulled away. The dressage rider in the passenger seat felt a bit miffed that she had overlooked this obvious facility – easy enough to achieve through the use of mobile telephony – and so that very day had a portable PC with mobile modem installed in the lorry.

The following weekend, as luck would have it, both contingents were setting off to the same dressage competition, and again the lorry was at a traffic light when the snooty dressage rider spotted the old LandRover and double trailer. It was pulled over at the side of the road, with steam coming from above the loading ramp. On seeing this, the dressage rider got out of her beautiful lorry and knocked on the loading ramp of the tatty trailer.

After a few moments, the LandRover driver poked his head out from the side of the trailer from which the steam was coming. His head was dripping with water.

'I've installed a PC with internet access in my lorry,' said the dressage rider proudly.

The LandRover driver groaned in annoyance. 'You got me out of the shower to tell me THAT?'

★ Funny business

Once upon a time there was a breeder watching his herd of miniature Shetland ponies in a field by a lonely road. Suddenly a brand new Range Rover and trailer screeched to a halt next to him. The driver, a young man dressed in a Savile

Row suit, Gucci shoes, Ray-Ban glasses and a Hermes tie, rolled the window down and asked the breeder, 'If I guess how many animals you have out there, will you give one of them to me?'

The breeder looked at the young man, then looked at the ponies which were grazing beyond and said, 'All right.'

The young man parked the Range Rover, connected his notebook computer to his mobile phone, entered a NASA site, scanned the ground using his GPS, opened a data base and 60 Excel tables filled with algorithms, then printed a 150-page report on his high-tech mini-printer. He then turned to the breeder and said, 'You have exactly 103 animals here.'

The breeder answered, 'That's correct, you can have your pony.'

The young man let down a ramp from the rear of the trailer, took the animal and led it up inside.

The breeder looked at the young man and asked, 'If I guess your profession, will you let me have my pony back?'

The young man answered, 'Yes, why not?'

The breeder said, 'You are a management consultant.'

'How did you know?' asked the young man.

'Very simple,' answered the breeder. 'First you come here without being invited. Second, you charge me a pony to tell me something I already know. Third, you do not understand anything about what I do, because you took my Irish Wolfhound.'

★ Tender gender

A three-year-old girl had just been with her mother to see the neighbour's new-born foal. They went into the house and the little girl ran to find her daddy so she could tell him all about it.

'Tell me,' asked her father, 'is it a boy foal or a girl foal?'

'A filly,' replied the little girl.

'And how could you tell? Did your Mum ask Mrs Jenkins?' asked the father.

'No,' replied the little girl. 'Mum looked between the foal's back legs. I think it must be printed on its tummy.'

★ Bogged down

Two women were driving a small horsebox down a country lane on their way to collect a new horse from a dealer's yard. They came to a flooded patch in the road and the lorry became bogged down. After a few fruitless minutes of trying to push and shove the lorry out by themselves, they saw a young farmer coming down the lane on a large tractor.

He stopped when he saw the women in trouble and offered to pull the lorry out for £50. The women accepted gratefully, and minutes later the lorry was pulled clear. The farmer turned to the women and said, 'You know, yours is the tenth vehicle I've helped out of there today.' The women looked around at the fields incredulously.

'When do you have time to work on your farm? At night?' asked one of the women.

'No,' the young farmer replied seriously, 'Night is when I pump water all over the road.'

★ Head girls' comments on working pupils' progress reports

'I would not allow this working pupil to breed.'

' Works well when under constant supervision and cornered like a rat in a trap.'

'When she opens her mouth, it seems it is only to change whichever foot was previously there.'

'He would be out of his depth in a leaking water trough.'

'This young lady has delusions of adequacy.'

'He sets low personal standards and then consistently fails to achieve them.'

'This working pupil is depriving a village somewhere of an idiot.'

'Not the sharpest hoofpick in the grooming kit.'

'Probably has an IQ of around room temperature.'

'A photographic memory but with the lens cap stuck on.'

'Bright as the inside of the tackroom in a power cut.'

'Donated his brain to science before he had finished using it.'

'The bell has gone, judges are waiting, but she's still on the ground doing the girth up.'

'Has two brains: one is lost, the other is out looking for it.'

'If he were any more stupid, we could slice him up and put him in with the hard feeds in winter.'

'If you give her a penny for her thoughts, you'll get change.'

'One dandy brush short of a grooming kit.'

'Wheel is turning, but the hamster is dead.'

'The horses would follow him anywhere, but only out of morbid curiosity.'

★ Stable quiz

Two jockeys, a racing trainer and a young stable lad were chatting in the tackroom while waiting for a hailstorm to end. The storm went on and on and eventually all were getting bored.

'I know,' said the trainer. 'Let's do a quiz.' The others agreed and the trainer racked his brains for a question that wouldn't be too taxing. 'Okay,' he said, 'I'll buy a pint for the first one who answers this one correctly. Complete the phrase: Old MacDonald had a ...'

'House!' shouted the first jockey.

'No, that's not quite right,' smiled the trainer. 'Let's try again. Old MacDonald had a ...'

'Stable!' yelled the second jockey.

'No,' said the trainer, 'that's not quite right either. Let's have another go. Old MacDonald had a ...'

'Farm!' shrieked the stable lad.

'Well done!' said the trainer. 'And for another pint, how do you spell that?'

The three contestants looked at each other blankly, then the stable lad piped up.

'I know,' he said triumphantly. 'E-I-E-I-O!'

★ De-bagged

In a small village, farmers, huntspeople and landowners of the community had got together to discuss some important issues. About midway through the meeting, the wife of one of the farmers stood up and spoke her piece.

One of the old hunt servants stood up and said, 'What does she know about anything? I would like to ask her if she knows what a horse's tail looks like?'

Quick as a flash, the woman replied, 'Take off your trousers, sir, and check for yourself!'

★ Rich or what?

An English visitor was invited to tour the racing stables of a wealthy Saudi-Arabian billionaire. They were incredibly luxurious – the beds were so deep you couldn't see a single horse below the neck.

★ Alms for the poor

The seven-year-old daughter of a highly successful dressage rider attended a Pony Club camp on her sweet little Welsh Mountain pony. Although the child had a wonderful time, the mother, who had watched the group lessons with a highly critical eye, was unimpressed.

At the camp barbecue on the last day, the little girl went up to the instructor who had taken her ride and thanked her for giving such enjoyable lessons.

'Well, that's really nice of you, Abigail,' smiled the instructor.

'And when I grow up, Miss Simpson, I'm going to give you some money,' said the little girl.

The instructor was puzzled. 'But there's no need! Why ever would you want to do that?'

'Because,' replied the little girl, 'my Mum said you're the poorest instructor she's ever seen.'

★ Towing

A passing motorist skidded his car off the road in a lonely area. Luckily a local farmer came to help with his big, strong Shire horse, named Freddy. He hitched Freddy up to the car and yelled 'Pull, Ernie.' Freddy didn't move.

Then the farmer shouted, 'Pull, Bertie, pull!' Freddy didn't respond.

Once more the farmer commanded, 'Pull, Charlie, pull!' Still nothing happened.

Then the farmer nonchalantly said, 'Pull, Freddy, pull!' And the horse dragged the car out of the hedge with ease.

The motorist was very appreciative, and very intrigued. He asked the farmer why he called his horse by the wrong name three times.

The farmer said, 'Oh, Freddy is blind. If he had thought he was the only one pulling, he wouldn't even have tried!'

★ Luxury wrong

A British groom from deepest rural Suffolk was sent by his employer to accompany a young racehorse which had just been sold to a highly successful yard in Kentucky, USA. The groom was astounded at the luxury of the loose boxes when he was shown around them and invited to choose one for his equine companion. The first one he saw was equipped with deep rubber flooring, automatic water cooler, air conditioning, central heating, infra-red lamps, rich wood panelling and gold-plated fixtures. But the American head lad said no, he couldn't have that one for his horse, it was the feedstore.

★ English signs found in foreign equestrian centres

FRANCE
'Before riding please leave your values in the office.'

AUSTRIA
'Not to perambulate the floors of the cafeteria in the boots of equitation.'

FORMER USSR
'Here there will be a exhibition of equestrian art by dozens of Soviet Republic painters and sculptors these were executed over the past two years.'

GERMANY
'In case of fire, do your utmost to alarm the stable manager.'

SWITZERLAND
'It is strictly forbidden on the centre's camping site that

people of different sex, for example men and women, live together in one tent unless they are married with each other for this purpose.'

HOLLAND
'All horses shod by the latest methodists.'

BELGIUM
'Take one of our horse-driven city tours we guarantee no miscarriages.'

TURKEY (donkey rides)
'Would you like to ride on your own ass?'

SWEDEN (saddler)
'Bridles made for customers from their own hides.'

JAPAN (diversion off bridleway)
'Stop ride sideways.'

LUXEMBURG
'If this is your first visit to XXX Equestrian Centre you are welcome to it.'

SPAIN
'Please do not feed the horses – if you have any suitable food give it to the groom on duty.'

ITALY (on water hose)
'If you want more water for hose horses' legs please control yourself.'

MAJORCA
'English well talking here speeching American.'

★ Experience

Several weeks after a young apprentice stable lad had been hired, he was called into the head lad's office. 'What is the meaning of this?' the head lad asked. 'When you applied for this job, you told us you had five years' experience. Now we discovered this is the first job you've ever held.'

'Well,' the young lad replied, 'in your advertisement you said you wanted somebody with imagination.'

★ Bridal

A showjumper and his bride asked the hotel receptionist for a room, telling him they just got married that morning.

'Congratulations!' said the receptionist. Looking at the showjumper, he asked, 'Would you like the bridal then?'

'No, thanks,' said the showjumper. 'I'll just hold her by the ears till she gets the hang of it.'

★ Dude ranch

A young man who wanted to appear 'macho' when visiting a dude ranch in the United States, went out walking with one of the hired hands. As they were walking through the yard, the visitor tried starting a conversation. 'Say,' he said, 'what a great bunch of Mustangs.'

The hired hand replied, 'Not "bunch", but "herd".'

'Heard what?'

'Herd of Mustangs.

'Sure, I've heard of Mustangs. There's a big bunch of 'em right over there.'

★ Document

An elderly horse breeder answered a knock on his door one morning. An electricity company worker handed him a piece of paper stating that the electric company intended to run pylons and power lines through his field.

The elderly man said, 'No, you may not.'

'Legally, this document says we can,' replied the worker.

As the worker turned and left, returning to his co-workers in the field, the elderly man went to his stable block and turned his very large Suffolk Punch stallion out into the field.

As the stallion galloped angrily towards the workers in the field, the elderly man shouted, 'There! Show him your document!'

★ Pony express

At a post office in Milwaukee, USA, a woman complained to the attendant that a Pony Express rider could get a letter from Milwaukee to St Louis in two days, and now it takes three. 'I'd like to know why,' she ranted.

The attendant thought a moment and then suggested, 'Well, the horses are a lot older now.'

★ How now, brown cow

A group of senior citizens were taken by bus to visit a large farm some 40 miles from the city where they all lived. Being urban people they weren't familiar with country ways, and were astonished at these strange surroundings and creatures.

One elderly lady strode up to the fence between the yard and a paddock and saw something she thought was quite remarkable. The farmer was nearby, so she called him over. 'Excuse me,' she said, 'but why doesn't this cow have any horns?'

The farmer stroked his chin for a moment, then said, 'Well, my dear, cattle can do an awful lot of damage with their horns. Sometimes we keep the horns trimmed down with a hacksaw. In other cases, with young ones, we put a few drops of acid where the horns would grow through and that stops them developing altogether. On the other hand, of course, some breeds of cattle don't grow any horns at all.'

'Hmmm, that's very interesting,' said the elderly lady. 'In which category is this one, then?'

'Well, my dear,' said the farmer, 'the reason why this cow has no horns is because it's a New Forest pony.'

★ Tall tales

A businessman was driving along a country road and felt hungry. As he was miles from the nearest town or village he couldn't stop at a pub or café. However, he remembered that he had some sandwiches and a can of fruit drink in the back of his car, so he stopped and fetched these from the boot. As he was leaning against the car eating a sandwich, a horse trotted up to the fence by the road and began talking.

'Did you know,' said the horse, 'that I'm a star showjumper? I've won thousands in prize money and have won all the major showjumping competitions in Europe. Even the Puissance at Olympia, and the European Individual Championship.'

The businessman dropped his sandwich in alarm as he listened to the horse. Eventually he recovered his senses sufficiently and decided to visit the yard at the far end of the field, where the horse came from. The horse trotted alongside him as he hurried to the tackroom door. When they got there, a woman came out. Not wishing to waste any time, the businessman said to her, 'I would like to buy this horse, and I will give you £100,000 for him.'

The woman agreed without any hesitation, and as the businessman began to walk away, he stopped suddenly. 'Why,' he asked, 'were you so eager to sell your horse?'

The woman snorted. 'Because he's a ruddy liar. He's never won a showjumping competition in his life.'

★ Ten reasons to take up dressage

1. I found flea-racing too exciting.

2. I enjoy wearing full formal riding kit, even on hot summer days.

3. I've always wanted to ride around in circles getting shouted at.

4. I want to subject my friends and family to hours of my half-pass on video.

5. My osteopath needs a new car.

6. I wanted to find a place where my husband wouldn't go (the yard).

7. I hate spending cold winter mornings snuggled up in bed and winter evenings by a warm fire.

8. My lawyer thinks it would be good practice for me to have three judges.

9. I've always wanted to look a judge in the eye and say 'Piaffe'.

10. I have far too much money in my bank account.

★ Hello, Vicar

The local Vicar had decided to buy a pony for his daughter, and after searching through endless advertisements finally found one that sounded appropriate. He set off to see the pony at a yard some miles away.

'Now this pony,' said its owner, 'is as gentle and kind as you could want. He will stand quietly even if he isn't tied up. He will do anything you ask of him. He genuinely hasn't any vices or bad characteristics at all. He doesn't bite or kick, and he listens to everything you say.'

'Goodness me,' sighed the Vicar. 'If only he were a member of my congregation.'

★ How to ...

Get your mare to go into labour – finally give up and crawl into bed at 3 am.

Get your mare to come into season – take her to a show.

Ensure your mare gets in foal first time – wrong stallion leaps fence at stud.

Ensure your mare has that near-perfect filly you've always wanted – sell her before she has foaled.

Cure your horse of constipation – load him into a freshly cleaned trailer.

Cure your horse of lethargy – take him into an in-hand showing class.

Get your horse to wash his/her own feet – scrub out the water trough and fill it with fresh water.

Bring on a spell of freezing weather – clip your horse before your winter turnout rug is back from the cleaners.

Make it rain – mow your hay fields.

★ Looking good

An American horse lover was driving by a farm in Indiana when he spotted a beautiful horse. He stopped, found the farmer, and said, 'Your horse looks really good. I'll give you a thousand dollars for him.'

'He don't look so good, and anyway he's not for sale,' grunted the farmer in reply.

'Okay,' said the man, 'I think he looks incredibly good, so I'll give you two thousand dollars for him.'

'Aw, he don't look so good,' replied the farmer, 'but if you want him that badly, all right, you can have him.

The man came back later that day with his lorry, loaded the horse and took him home. The next morning he was on the phone to the farmer, shouting with fury. 'You old so-and-so,' he ranted, 'that horse is blind! You swindled me!'

'No, I didn't,' replied the farmer. 'I told you he don't look so good.'

★ Advantages of husbands over horses

Husbands cost less to shoe than horses.

Feeding a husband doesn't require you to break your fingernails tying up a haynet, and you can feed a husband in warm surroundings and good light.

If a husband goes lame, he can usually still work.

If a husband gets tummy ache, he doesn't have to be walked around a cold yard until the vet arrives.

If you're having trouble catching a husband, you can run almost as fast as he does.

Husbands usually pay at least a proportion of their feed and medical bills.

Husbands normally say they're sorry when they step on your foot.

Husbands get into a vehicle with no problems.

Husbands don't boxwalk, shout and sweat up if they're left alone while you take the other horse out.

Husbands usually go out and get someone else to clip them, so you don't have to.

★ Advantages of horses over husbands

If your relationship with a horse doesn't work out you can sell it or put it out on loan.

You're never likely to endure having your horse's mother to stay for Christmas.

You don't have to worry whether your children will look like your horse.

You don't have to iron saddle cloths, numnahs, cotton girths or turnout rugs.

If you put on weight and get too heavy for your horse, you simply buy a bigger horse.

Horses don't smell terrible when they're sweating.

Horses, in the main, have no interest whatsoever in football, beer, pubs and dirty old motorbikes.

It's entirely up to you whether your horse stays fit and slim.

Horses don't like watching endless sport on television.

Horses may go grey as they get older, but they never go bald.

Horses love you just the same whether your hair and makeup are done or not.

★ S*d's law

No one ever takes notice of how you ride until you fall off in front of them.

The least talented horse on the yard is the one that eats the most, needs shoeing once a month and has to see the vet every three weeks.

The degree of your horse's misbehaviour will be in direct proportion to the number of people watching.

It's always the newest, most expensive rug that gets torn on barbed wire.

The cheapest, nastiest rugs never get damaged and never wear out.

The horse or pony you like the least can never be sold and will outlive you.

Clipper blades will go dull and need replacing when your horse is half-clipped.

If you go to check your horse on your way out for the evening dressed in clean clothes, he will fling slobber all down you from twenty feet away.

Your stables will fall down if you untie even one piece of baler twine.

Hoofpicks always grow legs and run away.

If you fall off your horse you will always land on the same part of your body that you injured last time.